Inspiring Courage
Women in Law and Public Advocacy

Jean Miranda Fleming

Table of Contents

Fight for the things that you care about, but do it in a way that will lead others to join you.

— Ruth Bader Ginsburg

Chapter 1. Introduction

Are you ready to immerse yourself in a world of tenacity, ambition, and groundbreaking leadership? Our Special Report, "Inspiring Courage: Women in Law and Public Advocacy," invites you to experience firsthand the unassailable bravery and resilience of women who have paved the way in fields often dominated by men. In this special report, we delve into the lives of these remarkable females, their trials, travails, and triumphs, providing exclusive insights into the impact they have made on not just law and advocacy, but society as a whole. Every page serves as a testament to their enduring spirit and their ability to shatter glass ceilings, advocating for justice while inspiring future generations. Get ready to be inspired, engaged, and motivated to make a difference by these incredible women. Discover, celebrate, and absorb the adventure of being a woman in law and advocacy with this riveting collection!

Chapter 2. Trailblazers: The Early Women in Law and Advocacy

Our journey into the history of women in law and advocacy begins by paying homage to the fearless trailblazers who laid down the groundwork, enduring grueling and often, gut-wrenching circumstances to give women the precedents we proudly rely on today.

2.1. The Dawn of Women's Legal Journey

The start of the women's legal odyssey can be traced back to the mid-nineteenth century. It was a period of dramatic change and societal evolution, thanks in no small part to the pioneering women who dared to step into the world of law. They boldly asserted their right to be recognized not just as equal citizens, but equal minds competent to interpret and influence the laws that governed their lives.

Themes of rebellion, defiance, and resilience run deep within these early narratives. These weren't just women striving for personal accomplishments; they were crusaders fighting for the rights of future generations. Beneath their legal caps and gowns dwelled hearts set ablaze with courage, unyielding in the face of adversity.

2.2. The Indomitable Myra Bradwell: A Burning Passion for Justice

In an era where women were expected to remain on society's sideline, Myra Bradwell was a standout figure. As a lawyer, editor, and publisher, Bradwell embodied tenacity and strength, with the power of her intellect earning her respect in a dominantly male field. While Bradwell is remembered primarily for her contributions as a legal journalist, her personal journey showcases the formidable obstacles she had to overcome.

Bradwell's saga took a crucial turn in 1869 when she applied to the Illinois bar. Despite passing her examinations with flying colors, her application was denied solely on the grounds of her being a woman. This spurred Bradwell on a legal crusade that spanned nearly a decade.

Taking her case to the United States Supreme Court, Bradwell contended for not just her right to practice law, but for the rights of all women to participate in the public sphere. Unfortunately, the high court was neither ready nor willing to view women as equals and she endured a devastating defeat.

This setback did not deter her; it stoked the flame of her conviction. Though she could not personally reap the fruits of her relentless struggle, in 1890, the Illinois Supreme Court decided to acknowledge her perseverance and granted her the license to practice law.

Bradwell's narrative, marked by remarkable resilience, sparked a wave of women seeking legal careers, laying the foundation for the fight against occupational segregation.

2.3. Belva Lockwood: An Unyielding Spirit

Belva Lockwood serves as another stellar example of female tenacity in the early legal realm. Despite repeated rejection from law schools, Lockwood persevered, ultimately gaining admittance to the National University Law School (now George Washington University Law School).

In 1879, Lockwood achieved a significant milestone — she became the first woman to be admitted to the bar of the United States Supreme Court.

This singular achievement epitomized her unconquerable spirit, but Lockwood's vision stretched beyond her personal journey. Recognizing the importance of political activism, she campaigned vigorously for women's suffrage, defining herself not merely as a lawyer but an advocate for women's rights.

The impact of her achievements is immeasurable, providing women with a profound belief in their capabilities in the inherently biased legal domain.

Both Bradwell and Lockwood are representative of the countless women who staved off the weight of societal prejudices. Laws and societal norms may have been against them but their conviction didn't falter. Their daunting path carved out a space for women in law and advocacy.

2.4. Impact and Legacy

The ripple effects of these early trailblazers' determination are felt even today. They challenged the embedded discrimination within the legal profession, setting a precedent for equal rights. Today, women account for approximately 37% of lawyers in the US, and this number is continually increasing, largely due to the relentless determination of these first women in law and advocacy.

Yes, there is still work to do. We still have mountains to climb before we can say we've reached gender equality within the legal profession. But as we forge ahead, let's not forget the fearless women who dared to venture into the then intimidating realm of law and advocacy. They've set a powerful example of tenacity, resilience, and courage, urging us to keep fighting; to never tire until we've reached the peak.

These women are more than just signposts in the annals of legal history; they are reminders of the power of defiance, the sense of purpose, and the courage to challenge the status quo. The legacy they left behind continues to guide us, inspiring us to push boundaries and shatter ceilings to pave the way for a more equitable world.

Chapter 3. The Legal Labyrinth: Struggles of Women and Miles Conquered

The legal profession holds a distinct position in society due to its dynamic and ever-evolving nature that penetrates, manipulates, and reshapes the value diffusion within societal constructs. As a discipline concerning the dispensation of justice, it requires the representation of varied perspectives, the plausibility of diverse arguments, and an egalitarian ethos that transcends the boundaries of class, race, and importantly, gender.

3.1. The Genesis of Gender Imbalance in Law

Indeed, acknowledging the struggles of women in law requires a thorough exploration of the historical roots of gender imbalance. Law, an industry once deemed inappropriate for women, traced its earliest female legal practitioners back to the all-encompassing defiance against patriarchal norms and stereotypes. Despite challenges related to societal mores, educational disparities and economic barriers, early women in law resisted the gendered confines of their era. They sought educational opportunities and broke through institutionalized biases to make significant strides for their gender.

The initial struggles rippled across surmounting barriers such as the right to a legal education, admission to the bar, and equal opportunities for employment. Most law schools barred women or were hesitant to admit them. The few brave early women legally educated, often self-taught, faced rejections and refusals when they applied to be part of the bar.

3.2. The Trials and Triumphs of Pioneering Legal Women

History is replete with stories of phenomenal women demonstrating unparalleled tenacity. The likes of Arabella Mansfield, the first woman admitted to a state bar in 1869 in Iowa, and Charlotte E. Ray, the first African-American female lawyer admitted to the District of Columbia Bar in 1872, provide illuminating examples of persevering through gender and racial biases. These women became the driving force behind a much-needed transformation in the legal landscape.

Another peculiarity that differentiates the struggles of women in law is the intersectionality of challenges. Women of color, LGBTQIA+ women, and women from other marginalized communities witnessed amplified discrimination. Their struggle was not merely against gender biases but also against racial, sexual, cultural, and social prejudices.

3.3. Parallels in the Modern Age: Persistent Barriers

One might question the relevance of these historical struggles in the modern era, an epoch symbolized by legal equality and supposedly free of gender bias. However, even today, the ghost of these bygone tribulations haunts the hallowed halls of legal institutions. Women in law, although no longer pioneering as the firsts, face similar challenges in forms of glass ceilings, gender pay gaps, bias in promotions and assignments, sexual harassment, and even disproportionate representation in law firm partnerships and judgeships.

3.4. The Journey of Women Conquering Miles in Law

Despite encountering such harsh obstacles, the spirit of women continues unabated. The progress made is akin to conquering miles in a journey fraught with adversities. Women have surged past barriers and have etched their names in the annals of history. They have made huge strides in law, yielding real change and acknowledging the integral role women continue to play in the legal profession.

The first female United States Supreme Court Justice Sandra Day O'Connor, the formidable Ruth Bader Ginsberg, or internationally celebrated human rights lawyer Amal Clooney, among countless other examples, showcase not just the victories in this long-winded crusade but equally underscore the countless battles that women are still relentlessly fighting.

Moreover, the recognition of women's rights and the push for gender equality have witnessed significant advancements in legislation. The monumental passing of the 19th amendment in the United States in 1920 granting women the right to vote was a direct consequence of tireless advocacy by women lawyers and advocates. Laws related to workplace discrimination, sexual harassment, reproductive rights, and many others have been shaped and reshaped by women who refused to accept the status quo.

3.5. Towards an Egalitarian Legal Landscape

The fight against gender-based discrimination is far from over. Women still encounter bias and prejudice at every juncture. However, the narrative isn't just about the struggles; it's also about the miles conquered.

It is a testament to the unnerving tenacity of women in law and public advocacy, who challenged and transcended barriers at every step. Their endeavors have opened doors, shattered glass ceilings, and set precedents. They have paved the way while ardent young visionaries continue to follow their lead.

The voyage of women in law has been an arduous one, filled with numerous trials and triumphs. Yet, the destination is an ideal—a legal turf marked by gender equality, shaped by the diverse voices of men and women alike, and epitomizing true justice. Until this utopia is reached, even as the miles increase, the struggle will persist, but, as history has shown, so will the determination of women to conquer them. The legal labyrinth thus continues to evoke the spirit of courage and the essence of resilience within every woman who dares to venture into its realm.

Chapter 4. Stainless Steel Ceilings: Overcoming Gender Bias and Discrimination

Historically, the perception and experience of women in law and advocacy have been akin to gazing upon a stainless steel ceiling, seemingly impenetrable and reflective of a construct not made for their ascent. Amid societal evolution, progressing from an era where women had scant representation in the domain of law, overcoming both explicit and implicit biases and discrimination has demanded steadfast resilience and unwavering courage. This chapter explores the persistent repercussions of gender bias in this field and recounts the arduous tales of countless women who, through sheer grit, have managed to challenge and mitigate these prevalent detriments.

4.1. Navigating the Matrix of Discrimination

Discrimination and gender bias in law and public advocacy roles serve as formidable barriers for women. While taking varied forms, these obstacles find their roots in longstanding cultural norms, institutional settings, or personal prejudices. Women advocates often face blatant discrimination in hiring and pay scale, while subtly prejudiced comments and preferential treatment underpin the covert instances of gender bias. This substantial problem doesn't only limit women's access to opportunities and growth but also serves as an invisible remnant of patriarchal systems in seemingly progressive environments. Layered on top are the compounded biases when aspects like race or sexuality intersect with gender, exacerbating struggles for women of color or belonging to the LGBTQ+ community.

4.2. Pioneering Pacesetters: Challenging the Status Quo

Just as water seeps through the smallest of cracks, some women have strived and managed to carve their way through this stainless steel ceiling, manifesting a sense of white-knuckle courage and unyielding determination. True pioneers like Ruth Bader Ginsburg, the late Supreme Court Justice, and Kamala Harris, the first female Vice-President of the United States, have chastised gender biases through their impressive work ethic and their unabashed demand for equality. Through their tenacious pursuits, they have been the 'cracks' in the stainless steel ceiling, opening avenues for other women to follow suit.

4.3. Deconstructing Gender Biases and Discrimination

To dismantle such a deeply ingrained structure, one must first scrutinize the underlying factors that contribute to these pervasive patterns actively. Stereotypical notions like women being too 'vulnerable' for the abrasive world of law or 'emotional' for the cold neutrality of justice underpin the misogynistic convictions that hinder women's progress. Acknowledging these biases and assumptions is the first step towards deconstruction, while concerted actions from individuals, organizations, institutions, and policymakers form the 'drill' that would bore holes in the stainless steel ceiling.

4.4. Beyond Personal Triumphs: Structural and Social Change

While celebrating women who have broken down barriers, it's

crucial to not overlook the necessity for overall systemic changes. Ensuring pay equity, fostering an inclusive work environment, utilizing affirmative action, and adopting family-friendly policies are some actions that can help align the field of law and advocacy with the precepts of gender equality. Simultaneously, sensitizing societies to shun gender biases and to respect women's contributions is imperative to cultivate a supportive environment that aids their progression rather than hinders it.

4.5. The Pledge of Perseverance: Moving Forward Despite Challenges

The path to overcoming gender bias and discrimination is certainly not a linear one, rather it's often speckled with setbacks and disappointments. Nevertheless, perseverance and unity among the women in this field serve as the bulwarks against adversities. Encouraging one another, staying fierce in conviction, and tenaciously fighting for what's right, the road ahead might seem daunting, but the journey traversed so far signals a promising future.

In conclusion, the task of overcoming this stainless steel ceiling, as seemingly insurmountable as it may appear, is not an impossible one. It requires, however, a combined and unremitting effort from all segments of society. By spotlighting the issue and proactively working towards eradicating it, we edge closer to a reality in which every woman willing to get into law and advocacy can do so sans deterring bias and prejudice, and with the rightful anticipation of achieving her fullest potential.

Chapter 5. Profiles of Courage: Pioneering Women in Law

The annals of legal history are marked by stoic resolve and relentless determination, and nowhere is this truer than in the legendary careers of pioneering women in law. Their lives are rich tapestries woven with perseverance, tenacity, and an unwavering dedication to justice.

5.1. The Vanguard: Early Women Attorneys

The early 20th century marked a crucial shift in the legal landscape of the world, ushering in the first wave of women attorneys. These women were trailblazers in the truest sense, shaping new paths and challenging the status quo in a world hitherto dominated by men.

Among the vanguard, the eminent name of Myra Bradwell springs forth. An indomitable spirit, Bradwell faced considerable obstacles in her endeavour to become the first woman lawyer in the United States. After qualifying for the bar in 1869, she was unceremoniously denied the right to practice on account of her gender. However, armed with unwavering resolve and fierce tenacity, Bradwell took her battle all the way to the US Supreme Court, thereby effectively catapulting the issue of gender equality into national consciousness.

5.2. The Modern Marvels: Mid-century Struggles

The mid-century years witnessed another wave of pioneering

women, defined by their prodigious abilities and tireless advocacy for justice. Among them stood women like Ruth Bader Ginsburg and Sandra Day O'Connor.

Ginsburg, the second woman to serve on the US Supreme Court, was renowned for her legal acumen and tireless advocacy for gender equality. Her meticulous and nuanced opinions have left a lasting impact on the American legal landscape. Battling gender discrimination in her personal and professional life, Ginsburg's lasting legacy is her unwavering commitment to the cause of equality.

The first woman Supreme Court Justice, Sandra Day O'Connor, carved out a unique trajectory, shattering the glass ceiling, and serving as a beacon for countless women aspiring to legal careers. O'Connor's judicious balancing of conservatism and pragmatism in her jurisprudence continues to significantly influence legal discourse in the US.

5.3. The Torchbearers: Lighting the Path Forward

The late 20th and 21st centuries brought forth a new wave of female legal luminaries, carrying the banner of justice into the modern era. Sonia Sotomayor, the first Hispanic and third woman appointed to the US Supreme Court, stands tall among these torchbearers.

Sotomayor's journey, from a modest upbringing in the Bronx to the hallowed corridors of the Supreme Court, is nothing short of inspirational. Her impactful decisions underscore her commitment to human rights and her dedication to public service.

Another gleaming torchbearer is Kimberlé Crenshaw, an American lawyer, philosopher, and leading authority on civil rights. Her groundbreaking work in critical race theory and coining of the term intersectionality has significantly broadened the contemporary discourse on identity politics and discrimination.

5.4. The Price of Pioneering: Unyielding Battles Fought

The journey of these pioneers was not without tribulations. Challenges were many and diverse - from societal prejudice to institutionalized discrimination. Each roadblock presented an opportunity for these women to push boundaries, challenge existing norms, and bring about meaningful shifts in the rigid structures of the law. Their journeys serve as a stark reminder that the path to equality is fraught with difficulties, yet the rewards of perseverance are profound and far-reaching.

In conclusion, the journey of pioneering women in law is a stirring narrative of resilience and a testament to their indefatigable spirit. The legal world, and indeed humanity at large, owes much to their courage, dedication, and tireless pursuit of justice. Their stories inspire and motivate, lighting a beacon for future generations of women in law. And in these profiles of courage, we find our collective roadmap for future progress towards a more equal, just, and equitable society.

Chapter 6. Pushing Boundaries: Women in Public Advocacy

In the historical landscape, women have constantly been at the forefront of pushing boundaries, taking a stand, and being an influential voice in public advocacy. Despite the undeniable challenges posed by patriarchal norms and ingrained gender stereotypes, their work has tremendously impacted various socio-political spheres, shaping legislation, policy reform, and societal understanding.

6.1. Breakthroughs in Public Advocacy

Public advocacy is unquestionably a verdant field, richly imbued with opportunities for change and advancement. It is a space where words turn into actions, and voices can echo powerfully, challenging inequities and championing initiatives for a more inclusive, equitable society. Women have played an intrinsic role in this sphere, successfully stirring dialogues, engaging stakeholders, weathering resistance, and effectuating sizable shifts in various realms.

In the early 20th century, women such as Susan B. Anthony, Elizabeth Cady Stanton, and Sojourner Truth paved the way for future change-makers. They were beasts of burden who etched into stone the very pathways subsequent generations would traverse in their quest for gender equality. Their fight for women's suffrage was a turning point in public advocacy, changing the course of history and setting the stage for women to engage more actively in political and public roles.

6.2. The Plaza of Diplomacy

Global diplomacy has been another forum where women have striven to make their mark. Historically, women diplomats such as Eleanor Roosevelt, who played a vital role in drafting the Universal Declaration of Human Rights, have demonstrated that women can, and do, wield significant influence on the diplomatic stage. Their contributions to shaping international relations, fostering peacekeeping dialogues, negotiating treaties, and addressing global issues are impressive and indeed groundbreaking. Modern-day women diplomats continue to pioneer changes, breaking gender stereotypes, and relentlessly advocating for gender-inclusive policy-making in their respective fields.

6.3. Media Platforms and Gender-based Advocacy

In an age where the media serves as a potent contributor to molding public perception, women have harnessed its power in advocacy work. Using various platforms—traditional press, social media, filmography, literature, music—they have been amplifying their voices and influencing societal narratives around systemic injustice and discrimination against women.

Gloria Steinem, a leading feminist journalist of the 1960s and 1970s, used her magazine to talk about issues affecting women, from reproductive rights to workplace discrimination. In the contemporary context, advocates and activists like Malala Yousafzai ingeniously employ social media platforms to bring awareness to issues about female education and child marriage.

Whether it is through hashtag campaigns or viral video content, women are pushing boundaries on the digital front, urging society to reconsider and reimagine gender dynamics.

6.4. The Corporate Staircase: Ascension and Influence

Women have also transcended barriers in the corporate world, emerging as influential figures in decision-making roles. While it is evident that gender disparity still exists, particularly in leadership positions, the advancements that women in the corporate sector have made are significant.

Women like Sheryl Sandberg, Facebook's COO, Rosalind Brewer, CEO of Walgreens Boots Alliance, and Mary Barra, CEO of General Motors, are testaments to the burgeoning empowerment of women in leadership roles. They not only present a challenge to gender stereotypes in the corporate world but also advocate for gender parity and provide a beacon of hope for aspiring female corporate leaders.

6.5. The (Never) Final Frontier: Unyielding Strides Ahead

Women in public advocacy are formidable players in societal and policy transformation. While their monumental strides are celebrated, it remains vitally important to acknowledge that their journeys are far from over. Despite substantial progression, gender disparity still persists, and women continue to face systemic challenges inherently woven into the societal fabric.

The women advocates from diverse backgrounds who lead public advocacy movements display unassailable courage, audacious spirit, and an unwavering tenacity. In demonstrating their capabilities, they are not only challenging the gender status quo but also setting a precedent for generations to come.

In conclusion, the realm of public advocacy represents an ongoing saga of women's steadfast determination and indomitable will. Their journey, marred by struggles yet decorated with triumphs, encapsulates an inspirational narrative of empowerment. It's the tale of quiet whispers turning into resounding roars, of boundaries transcending into horizons, and most importantly, of women taking the reins, becoming the change-makers they were always meant to be.

Chapter 7. The Intersectionality Challenge: Balancing Gender, Race, and Advocacy

In the multifaceted realm of law and public advocacy, the journey for women is nothing short of a Herculean task. If being a woman in these fields presents its unique set of challenges, belonging to a minority complicates the situation further by adding layered intersections of gender, race, ethnicity, or sexual orientation. This chapter endeavors to thoroughly explore these complexities, shedding light on the struggles women grapple with and the victories they have achieved in the face of intersectionality.

7.1. The Struggle with Identity: Layers of Intersectionality

Intersectionality, as a concept, is a theoretical framework that encapsulates the idea that multiple social identities - such as being female, Black, and a lawyer - intersect to create a whole that extends beyond the sum of its components. Kimberlé Crenshaw, who coined the term, aimed to challenge the dominant modes of thought that limit gender and race to mutually exclusive categories. She strove to stress the ways in which power structures and systemic oppression interact, exacerbate, and multiply each other within the lives of myriad individuals.

For women in the field of law and public advocacy, the realm of intersectionality fosters a dichotomy where they are expected to negotiate their professional career trajectory while simultaneously grappling with societal prejudices. In other words, their struggles do not stop at the gender divide, but are compounded by confrontations with racial bias. For instance, a Black woman attorney might grapple not only with gender bias, where her competence is questioned simply because of her sex, but also racial bias, where she is subjected to systemic racism which questions her suitability based on her skin color.

7.2. Achievements amidst Adversities: Intersectional Advocacy

Even amidst such seemingly insurmountable obstacles, many women have managed to break through the glass ceiling and paint the landscape of law and public advocacy with their indomitable spirit and relentless determination. Examples abound of this enthralling resilience - from Charlotte E. Ray, who in 1872, became the first African American female attorney in the United States, shattering both race and gender barriers, to Eleanor Roosevelt, who as the "First Lady of the World," championed civil rights, confronting the system of exclusionary and compounded prejudice.

Such women in law and public advocacy have also leveraged their intersectional identities to inform their advocacy work, aiming to eradicate systemic barriers and unfair norms that impinge upon marginalized groups. Their lived experiences have ignited their passion and provide them with a unique perspective, enabling them to sympathetically and empathetically advocate for others who experience similar intersectionality disparities.

7.3. Intersectionality-Informed Policy: A New Frontier

Indeed, the political and legal landscape is slowly but surely shifting towards acknowledging the influence of intersectionality. Several leading women advocates and lawmakers are working relentlessly to integrate intersectionality into policies and laws. By doing so they hope to create a more inclusive and encompassing legal system which takes into account the intricacies of intersectional identities and their associated disparities.

Key legislative movements and campaigns, such as the fight for equal pay - which is strikingly pronounced in the intersection of gender and race, where the gender pay gap widens substantially for Black, Hispanic, and Indigenous women - reflect the intention to incorporate a comprehensive intersectional lens to policy and law creation.

7.4. Encouraging Intersectionality in Advocacy: Future Directions

As the new dawn of intersectionality in advocacy begins to rise, there is an urgent need to foster an environment that not only acknowledges intersectionality but actively encourages it. Such inclusivity requires altering stereotypes, challenging biases, and instigating systemic changes to ensure women of all backgrounds can thrive in the realm of law and public advocacy.

Respecting intersectionality may also involve modifying training and education programs, adapting workplace cultures, and encouraging a more diversified representation within the higher echelons of professional hierarchies. By doing so, we can build a more accommodating environment for women who continue their fight against layered forms of discrimination.

In conclusion, the voyage of intersectional women in law and public advocacy exemplifies an inspiring story of resilience and innovation. Despite the adversity that layered prejudices bring, these women do not shy away from their identities. Instead, they embrace them and use their unique perspectives to fuel their work in advocacy. This chapter, therefore, serves as an homage to these audacious women who dared to challenge the status quo, paving the way for a new era of intersectionality-informed law and policy.

Chapter 8. Agents of Change: How Women Advocates Impact Legislation and Policy

For this chapter, we invite you to embark on a profound journey to explore the significant roles women have played as agents of change, shaping legislation and policy within the realms of law and public advocacy.

8.1. Pioneers of Change: Notable Women Advocates in History

Let's commence this exploration with the pioneers who set the stage for future women advocates. Susan B. Anthony, Elizabeth Cady Stanton, Alice Paul, to name only a few, sketched an incredible beginning in women's advocacy, fighting arduously for women's suffrage, striking at the roots of gender inequality embedded in the U.S. Constitution. Against the backdrop of a male-dominated society, these courageous women instigated dramatic public debates, challenged the status quo, and effectuated monumental legislation alterations, culminating in the landmark 19th Amendment granting women the right to vote.

8.2. Shaping Legal Framework: Women's Impact on Legislation

Indeed, women involved in advocacy have prominently dissented against biased legislations that failed to accommodate women's interests. Their efforts have birthed transformative legislation pieces.

Ruth Bader Ginsburg, the second woman to serve on the Supreme

Court, overturned several regressive rulings favoring gender discrimination through her tenacious advocacy for equal rights, making her an icon in the fight against gender discrimination.

Consider the case of the Violence Against Women Act (VAWA), championed by then-Senator Joe Biden but significantly raised and supported by female advocates pushing for legislative action against domestic violence – a glaring testament to the power of women advocates in influencing legislation.

8.3. Transitioning Advocacy to Policy: The Seismic Shifts Effected

Women advocates have also translated their causes into effective public policies, reshaping the societal landscape. The landmark case of Roe v. Wade, which affirmed a woman's legal right to have an abortion, was pushed into becoming a major U.S. policy by passionate advocacy from women's rights groups.

Moreover, advocacy for equal pay for equal work and the sustained fight against sexual harassment at workplaces have resulted in several policy adaptations that uphold women's rights, reshaping corporate cultures, and democratizing workplaces.

8.4. The Ripple Effects: Global Applications of Women-Influenced Legislation

Women's advocacy and the consequential legislation have not been limited to domestic boundaries. Globally, individuals like Malala Yousafzai have catalyzed dialogues about girls' right to education, galvanizing global support and policies favoring female education.

From women's rights to climate change, international legislation influenced by women advocates has often proved groundbreaking, fueling movements and legislative changes across the globe.

8.5. The Path Ahead: Continual Impact on Legislation and Policy

Despite the significant strides made by women advocates, there's no denying the long path ahead remains strewn with challenges. Yet, these trailblazing women continue to illuminate the way, pressing for change within legislations and policies, advocating for equal rights, environmental justice, health care reforms, and much more.

Undoubtedly, fulfilling the promise of equality and justice will require relentless advocacy, but as history has demonstrated, women advocates are unwavering agents of change, persistently effecting significant shifts in legislation and policy.

Through the exploration of this chapter, one can surmise the collective power of women in driving public advocacy and legislation, overcoming societal constructs and bias, rewriting rules, and echoing change across the world. Certainly, their journey serves as a tribute to every woman with the spirit of an advocate, pressing on against the odds and influencing the tenor of the times. It stands as a testament to the fact that not just in law, but in every realm, women can, and indeed, have been agents of change, shaping legislation and public policy, regardless of the barriers they've had to overcome.

Chapter 9. Empowering Tomorrow: Inspiring the Next Generation of Women Advocates and Lawyers

In featuring remarkable women who have made indelible marks in the realm of law and public advocacy, it is imperative we probe into the ways their legal and advocacy efforts build bridges towards a brighter future. This section underscores their missions, strategies, and visions for ensuring the continuation of the fight for justice, equality and improvements in legislation affecting women and marginalized groups. Let's delve into the rich tapestry of their tactics for inspiring, enabling, and empowering the next generation of talented women to become trailblazing advocates and respected members of the legal profession.

9.1. Trail of Inspiration

The spirit of women, artists of audacious metamorphosis, has always been notable for its capacity to inspire others. As such, female lawyers and public advocates act as catalysts, using their own triumphs to evoke motivation in others, guiding aspiring women lawyers to navigate the labyrinthine legal profession traditionally dominated by men. These women are torchbearers, their awe-inspiring courage blossoming as a beacon of hope - a lighthouse guiding younger generations to chunks of opportunities and troves of possibilities.

9.2. Strategies for Emancipation

Beyond being sources of inspiration, successful women in law and advocacy, with their wealth of experience, have configured a multiplicity of strategies aimed at promoting and cultivating new generations of women in their fields. From structured initiatives such as mentorship programs and internships, to offering scholarships for aspiring female law students, these women are cultivating a nurturing environment that breaks the stereotypes, facilitating the rise of future successors in the field of law and advocacy.

9.3. Mentorship and Internships

An excessive number of these women have shared the necessity of having a mentor, someone to provide guidance, encouragement, and career advice. Many of these pioneers have become mentors themselves, offering their proteges a solid foundation paved with their wisdom and experiences. They also work with various law firms, nonprofits, and advocacy groups to provide internships. These internships act as stepping stones enabling aspirants to garner the experience and connections needed in their chosen field.

9.4. Scholarships and New Opportunities

Another worthwhile mention is the introduction of numerous scholarships aimed at assisting aspiring female lawyers with their financial burdens. This stride has opened up numerous channels and opportunities otherwise reserved for a privileged few. The provision of such scholarships seeks to rectify the imbalances that have persisted in post-secondary education allowing more women to pursue legal education.

9.5. Nurturing Spaces

Creating safe and nurturing spaces for open discussion and support is vital in a field that can be taxing and fraught with challenges. The establishment of various networks, forums, and societies built around the interests of female law students and advocates has served to create supportive communities that are instrumental in fostering the growth and development of future women leaders in legal and public advocacy spheres.

9.6. Vision of the Future

The trailblazing women in law and public advocacy don't just look at what's feasible right now, they look at the landscape of the future. They envision a realm where the scales of justice and advocacy are balanced, regardless of gender, ethnicity, or social standing. Aware that their struggle is part of a long journey, they consistently ideate and innovate in order to achieve long-term goals. Leaving a dynamic and inclusive society that fosters continual growth and development for women in law is also their shared vision.

In conclusion, the pioneering women who have forged a path in law and public advocacy are not only creating revolutionary changes, but they are also devoted to shaping the legal landscape for generations to come. They recognize the imperative nature of guiding, supporting, and mentoring the new age of women lawyers and advocates to guarantee a continuum of justice, advocacy and leadership. Their unwavering commitment to this cause illuminates the path for others, nurturing the seeds of courage and resilience in young women who desire to be part of this legacy. Through their efforts, they persist in creating ripples of change, each ripple magnifying into waves that set the stage for the future of law and public advocacy.

Chapter 10. The Power of Sisterhood: Networks and Support Systems in Law and Advocacy

In the challenging, competitive, and often male-dominated spheres of law and public advocacy, the power of sisterhood has always served as both an enduring constant and force multiplier for women. Found within these networks and support systems are unique dynamics fuelled by collective aspirations, shared experiences, and mutual accountability that vividly underline the significance of 'sisterhood.' This chapter will take you on an in-depth exploration of this theme, offering an insightful perspective on the transformative power that female solidarity, comradery, and mentorship bring to the table in these professions. It will provide extensive accounts of various network structures, their method of functioning, the various ways they cater to professional development, and the intrinsic support they offer to women in law and advocacy.

10.1. The Making of a Sisterhood-Dominant Network

Women's networks in law and advocacy, often known as 'women's circles,' originate from the recognition of shared experiences and mutual objectives. These dynamic groups operate primarily on the mechanics of mutual empowerment, mentorship, and accomplishment sharing. Through a detailed examination of the formation process, we'll scrutinize the common elements that serve as cornerstones to these groups: identification and recognition of collective struggles, acknowledgement of shared aspirations, a strong desire for equality, mutual aid, and cooperation.

10.2. Relevance and Impact of Sisterhood in Law and Advocacy

Our careful examination of these networks will bring to light the outstanding role sisterhood plays in the law and advocacy fields, focusing particularly on instances where collective female strength helped an individual, or even an entire generation, advance. Drawing upon real-life narratives, we'll showcase the benefits of such support systems, ranging from tackling workplace discrimination, coping with career transitions, to navigating the complex matrix of work-life balance and aspirations for leadership roles.

10.3. Fanning the Flames: Mentorship and Role Modelling in Legal Professions

This sub-chapter delves into the multifaceted role of mentorship within women's legal and advocacy networks. From sharing advice related to professional growth, breaking down barriers to counseling on personal development, female mentors wield great influence within these communities. Through extensive dialogue and first-hand narratives, we illuminate the crucial role these mentors play in transferring knowledge, wisdom, and experience, shaping the careers of many aspiring female lawyers and advocates.

10.4. Intersectionality and its Influence on Sisterhood Support Circles

Intersectionality must be examined within the broader context of networking and support provision among women in law and advocacy. By inspecting the crucial role intersectionality plays within these networks, we present a clearer snapshot of how these sisterhood structures contribute to the broader fight for justice and equality, beyond gender alone.

10.5. Challenges and Frontiers: The Future of Women's Networks in the Legal and Advocacy Sphere

Endeavoring to map out the future trajectory of women's circles in the legal profession, we'll highlight emerging trends and challenges that abound. Through a critical lens, we'll assess how evolving expectations, generational gaps, technology, and globalization dramatically influence the dynamics within these networks.

In revealing the intricacies of sisterhood in the realms of law and advocacy, we hope to shed light not only on the challenges women face, but also how solidarity, mentorship, and mutual support among them serve as vital aids in overcoming these hurdles. The power of sisterhood and the networks it fosters are more than just support systems; they are life-affirming testament to what women can achieve collectively in the face of daunting odds. As we journey into the future, let us celebrate this power and harness its potential to drive further change in the realms of law and public advocacy.

Chapter 11. Ongoing Struggles and Future Frontiers: Where We Stand and Where We Are Headed

As we turn the pages of history, tracing our path through the shifting sands of time, we discover the tales of courageous pioneers, trailblazers who bravely ventured into the male-dominated terrain of law and public advocacy. They charted new paths and shattered countless obstacles, illuminating the path for future generations of women. But the march towards equality, towards a world devoid of gender-based prejudice and discrimination, is far from over. The mission thus remains half-accomplished, the battle half-won.

11.1. The Ongoing Struggles

On careful inspection, the terrain traveled thus far reveals latent fissures that mark the challenges faced by women in these fields today. For every celebrated success story, countless trials and tribulations lie beneath the surface, a testament to the battles that remain to be fought. Systemic gender inequalities persistently lurk in these traditionally male-centric domains, presenting roadblocks and glass ceilings that hinder women's progression.

Workplace discrimination, gender-based bias, and unabated stereotypes continue to tamper with equal opportunities and fair treatment, rendering the professional atmosphere fraught with its own set of unique challenges. This is accompanied by the looming threat of harassment, an unsettling experience shared by numerous women across sectors, who are forced to maintain their resilience in the face of disparagement. Unequal pay wages for equal work, a struggle symbolizing the economic marginalization of women, is another pressing issue that demands urgent rectification.

Grasping this cognizance of the myriad struggles women endure in law and public advocacy, it becomes apparent that the vestiges of a patriarchal society continue to cast a long shadow over our present, echoing in the enduring struggles of professional women.

11.2. Navigating Future Frontiers

Turning towards tomorrow, we regard the horizon with a scrutinizing gaze, mapping the yet unchartered territories that await our footsteps. As formidable as these myriad challenges may appear, they pave the way for newer arenas of intervention and possibilities waiting to unfold.

The advent of technology has ushered in exciting opportunities and unique challenges alike in the realm of law and public advocacy. The emergence of cyber-law, intellectual property rights, AI in legal practice, digital forensics, and similar fields present women with a fresh avenue of simultaneous challenges and opportunities, offering arenas to exert influence and consolidate their position.

As diversity becomes a pertinent conversation in professional spaces, it becomes more imperative to stress the importance of fulfilling the demands of intersectionality, fostering an inclusive environment that understands and respects the nuances of gender, race, ethnicity, sexual orientation, and more. It entails broadening the spectrum of advocacy, graduating from singular narratives of gender to a multidimensional dialogue, incorporating diverse perspectives and voices in the discourse of law and public advocacy.

The future also reserves the task of equipping the next generation with the necessary arsenal of knowledge, skills, and sensibilities to seamlessly wield influence in these demanding fields. An endeavor of such magnitude necessitates the proactive nurturing of education, mentorship, and networking opportunities.

11.3. Where We Stand and Where We Are Headed

At this crossroads, we stand with a heart full of courage and a spirit that refuses to die. We stand at the intersection of change and inheritance, at a precipice that looks back at hard-fought battles while gauging the scope of untraveled paths. We cherish the legacies of the women who forged paths when none existed and pay homage to their ceaseless struggles. Simultaneously, we are diligently crafting new narratives, weaving new threads into the tapestry of history, carrying forth their torch to break our share of glass ceilings.

As for the road ahead, we see it winding into the horizon, fraught with challenges, yet brimming with promise. A path stretched with unexplored territories and undreamed possibilities. Yet, our resolve remains unshakeable, our optimism unwavering.

This is where we stand and where we are headed. The dawn of a new era, where women not only flourish in the domains of law and public advocacy but redefine these very landscapes. A time where our voices reverberate in boardrooms, courtrooms, and everywhere in between. Ready to carry forward the baton handed over by the relentless pioneers, we brace ourselves for a journey teeming with challenges yet abundant in promise.

The future is ripe for another wave of unassailable leaders, poised to shatter existing norms and carve out spaces that are inherently inclusive, egalitarian, and empowering. And thus, we continue on our journey – a quest to turn the dream of equality from an abstract ideal into a concrete reality, etching the legacy of women in law and public advocacy into the annals of history forever.